Reproducible Diversity and Culture Icebreakers

Jonamay Lambert
Selma Myers
George Simons

HRD Press, Inc. • Amherst • Massachusetts

Published by: HRD Press, Inc.
22 Amherst Road
Amherst, MA 01002
1-800-822-2801 (U.S. and Canada)
413-253-3488
413-253-3490 (fax)
www.hrdpress.com

ISBN 978-1-61014-355-4

Production services by Jean S. Miller
Cover design by Eileen Klockars
Editorial services by Suzanne Bay

Table of Contents

Icebreakers

Icebreakers are generally short activities whose purpose is to introduce people to one another and involve the participants in the topic or theme of the training meeting or seminar. Psychologically, they turn the participants' attention away from the flow of other activities in which they have been engaged and "bring them into the room" where the new focus will be on intercultural interactions and learning.

For this reason, they are valuable even for groups where the participants know each other well and work together on a regular basis. Often the icebreaker activity will give them permission to begin talking about cultural factors that they had not previously been aware of but that have been or are present in the workplace.

A good icebreaker activity will make the trainer's subsequent work easier by opening the participants' minds to other perspectives on their intercultural interactions and set the mood for sharing and participation.

These activities are designed to be simple and nonthreatening in order to reach these objectives. As with all activities, the trainer must be sensitive to the culture of the participants when choosing and administering the opening icebreaker activity.

1 Coups and Faux Pas

Dr. George Simons, George Simons International
Mandelieu-la Napoule, France

Purpose

To open an intercultural training program and begin a discussion of how cultural differences affect us in work or daily life

Target audience

This activity is for groups starting to learn about working or doing business across cultures. It requires some experience abroad (for work or vacation) or experience interacting with people of other cultures. Group members should not be afraid to share personal experiences. Coups and Faux Pas can be used even if most of the people in the group already know one another or are an intact work group. If the group is larger than 16, subdivide it into smaller groups for introductions there.

Time

Allow 5 minutes to set up the activity and introduce yourself. Then allow 1½ to 2 minutes per person, plus a few minutes to debrief.

Materials and environment

Handout 1: "66 Ways We Differ" for each participant

Procedure

Include the handout in the course documentation or put one at each person's place before the start of the program.

Tell the participants that you are all going to introduce yourselves to one another in a special way by sharing

- cultural *faux pas*—a mistake made abroad or when working with people of another culture—or

- cultural *coup*—something that turned out well when you respected another's cultural values.

Tell them that scanning the handout "66 Ways We Differ" might help them think of an experience.

Demonstrate what you mean by introducing yourself with BOTH a *coup* and a *faux pas*. Here are examples I have used in the past:

- **Faux pas:** *I was leaving a restaurant on a winter's evening in Northern Germany when a man appeared at the door roundly cursing me. I asked my companion what was wrong. He told me that I had failed to close the door and that I often failed to close doors. (Accustomed to automatic doors in public buildings and used to open spaces and "open-door policies" in the United States, I failed to observe that Germans have more doors and close them for privacy and quiet more often than Americans do.)*

- **Coup:** *The flight attendant on a recent trip asked what we would like for dinner. The man next to me asked that his meal be kept for him until 6:00 p.m. I realized that the man was probably a Muslim fasting for the season of Ramadan, so I asked the flight attendant to hold my meal until the same time. I was rewarded with a very interesting conversation about what it felt like to be a Muslim living abroad and the many misunderstandings and prejudices that this man had experienced living in my country. (During Ramadan, people fast by abstaining from food, drink, and smoking until sunset. It would have been very impolite for me to eat right next to him while he was fasting.)*

Give participants a couple of moments to prepare. Remind them that they need only share **either** a *coup* or a *faux pas.* Then go around the room and allow each person to introduce him- or herself.

Debrief

Transition into the next part of the program by telling the group that when it comes to culture, often "We don't know what we don't know," and that we frequently learn only by making mistakes. Tie this into the theme of the course: "It is the purpose of the course to learn how to avoid making tragic mistakes when dealing with people different from ourselves and to learn how to turn our mistakes into successes."

Note: The handout can be used for later discussion. You might ask the participants to form small groups to discuss one or more of the items on the list and attempt to identify the various kinds of differences they experience in life or work.

[Handout 1 – page 1]

Instructions to Trainer: Edit or change this list to make it fit your group or the topics you are interested in exploring during the rest of the program.

66 Ways We Differ

1. How we define "proper" behavior
2. How and when we greet one another
3. What's considered common courtesy
4. What's polite or impolite
5. How closely we stand to one another
6. The holidays we celebrate and how we celebrate them
7. How we show respect and disrespect
8. How and when we use money, credit, and bartering
9. The range in which we negotiate
10. What is modest or risqué
11. What is embarrassing or shameful
12. What makes us feel good, and what depresses us
13. What makes us proud, and what shames us
14. What, when, and how we eat and drink
15. What we wear, and when and where we wear it
16. How we see and behave toward sickness and health
17. How and when we seek and use health services
18. What we find funny or sad
19. How and when we use means of transportation
20. What we buy and sell, and when, how, and with whom we do it
21. When, where, and how we sit and stand
22. If, how, and when we touch one another
23. What we believe
24. What we value
25. What makes "common sense"
26. What are worthwhile goals in life
27. What is beautiful or ugly
28. The nature of God and other religious beliefs
29. What we believe we need and don't need
30. Whether privacy is desirable or undesirable
31. Who makes what decisions, and in what circumstances
32. Whether a person is in control of his or her own life, or whether fate determines it

Reproduced from *Reproducible Diversity and Culture Icebreakers,* by Jonamay Lambert, Selma Myers, and George Simons, editors. Amherst, MA: HRD Press, 2014

33. What should be communicated directly, and what indirectly
34. What or who is clean or dirty
35. What language, dialect, and tone of voice we use
36. To whom we speak and to whom we do not speak
37. The role of the individual
38. The roles of men and women, and how each should behave
39. The roles of parents and children, and how each should behave
40. The importance of harmony in a group
41. The importance of competition between individuals
42. Social class
43. Educational levels
44. Hierarchy in business relationships
45. How time is understood and used
46. Whether schedules are important or unimportant
47. The importance of tradition and rituals
48. How often we smile, whom we smile at, and what it means when we smile
49. How strangers interact
50. How we interact with a person in authority
51. How we interact with a person serving us (e.g., in a restaurant)
52. Relationships and obligations between friends
53. Relationships and obligations toward extended family members and relatives
54. Facial expressions and other nonverbal behavior and gestures, and when they are used
55. Crowd or audience behaviors
56. The importance of preparing for the future
57. How we see old age and how we value elders
58. Whether conversation should be formal or informal
59. What should be said; what should be left unsaid
60. Whether, when, how, and with whom we make "small talk"
61. How we perceive what is friendly or unfriendly
62. How open or guarded we are with information
63. What behavior is ethical and what behavior is not ethical
64. How, whom, and how much we entertain
65. How or whether we take turns, stand in line, etc.
66. How often we change jobs or "move house," and where and why

And, there are many, many other ways in which we differ!

② See Differences and Similarities

Ann Houston Kelley, M.A., Nomadic Life Management Consultants
Voorschoten, The Netherlands

Purpose and learning objectives

This is an introductory activity for a cross-cultural or diversity training session. It is best used after a round of formal participant introductions and an overview of the training program and procedures. This activity allows everyone to see the similarities as well as the richness of the diversity in the group. Specifically, it enables

- individual participants to experience visually and experientially how they are like and how they are unlike their fellow participants;

- the group of participants as a whole to see what the group is and what it is not;

- the trainer(s) to start making connections with the participants around the topic of differences and similarities;

- the trainer(s) to find out more about the participants and what their experiences are related to the topic. In today's fast-paced business environment, getting useful pre-program background information about session participants is often a luxury. Internal corporate training departments are short-staffed, last minute substitutions are common, and participants are often "too busy doing their jobs" to complete and return a pre-program questionnaire (even by e-mail). Trainers can use the data from this exercise to customize and adapt their training design and make it more relevant to the audience.

Target audience

Participants in a cross-cultural or diversity training session. Size of group might be limited by the space available to move about in the room.

Time

30 to 45 minutes

Materials and environment

Enough free space in the training room for four to five subgroups of participants to stand comfortably for five minutes at a time in different parts of the room.

Procedure

1. Prepare a list of ten questions beforehand. It is essential that any questions asked be appropriate for the participants as well as the organizational and host national cultures where the training takes place. Questions should be about visible as well as invisible (e.g., experiential) differences and similarities within the group. Here are some examples:

    - *What is your region, country, or continent of origin?*

    - *Have you lived, studied, or worked outside of your country of origin?*

    - *Is English your first, second, third, or fourth language?*

    - *How many languages do you speak (one, two, three, four, five, or more)?*

    - *Have you worked only for (company sponsoring the training) or for other companies as well?*

    - *Please group yourselves by gender.*

2. Introduce the activity, telling the participants that they will find out more specifically who is in the group and see the diversity of experience they bring to the training program and the company. Differences and similarities among participants joining a session are both visible and invisible. Participants make assumptions about the group and their fellow participants whether they know them or not. These assumptions are often based on little or faulty data. It is important early in the training to start exploring the reality of these assumptions.

3. Ask participants to group themselves in various parts of the room in response to each question as you ask it.

4. Ask the questions one at a time. Follow up each question with further questions or observations, such as how the diversity in the group impacts "how the business gets done" or how it might affect the training group atmosphere. For example, with the question about English as a first, second, third, or fourth language, ask the people who speak English as a third or fourth language how it is to communicate with native speakers on the job, and vice versa. You can also comment on how tiring it might be for a non-native speaker to work or attend a training session in English. With the question about work experience, you can ask for observations about corporate culture. If there is a clear minority answering any question, you can ask how it is to be a member of such a small subgroup in the training program or organization (e.g., one or two female participants in a training group of mostly men).

Debrief

Comment on the process of uncovering some additional similarities and differences within the group and how that process will continue throughout the training program as well as back on the job. You can discuss how diversity affects the effectiveness of teams or organizations. Links can be made here or later on to how subgroup membership can influence attitudes, beliefs, and behaviors. Participants can be encouraged to use examples of differences in the group from this exercise in subsequent exercises.

Options

This exercise can be used with groups of participants who know one another well, as well as with groups of participants who do not know one another or only know one another slightly. With an intact work group, the assumptions about similarities and differences can be even more important to highlight. Trainers should vary their questions according to what issues seem to be particularly relevant for each group of participants (e.g., departmental or facility culture versus differences in national culture).

Resources

Tavistock group relations theory looks at how unconscious processes operate in groups and offers an interesting framework for looking at the role of subjective assumptions in a work group's (or training group's) ability to "get on with performing its task." Those subjective assumptions need to be surfaced and tested in order for the group to start working together more effectively. Systems exercises such as this can help surface these assumptions. For further reading on this topic, see the following:

Robert de Board, *The Psychoanalysis of Organizations*. New York: Routledge, 1978.

Arthur D. Colman, and W. Harold Bexton, editors. *Group Relations Reader 1*. Washington: A.K. Rice Institute, 1975.

Manfred F.R. Kets de Vries, *Organizations on the Couch*. Oxford: Jossey-Bass Limited, 1991.

Edgar Schein, *Organizational Culture and Leadership*. Oxford: Jossey-Bass Limited, 1985.

③ Where in the world do you come from?

Walt Hopkins, Castle Consultants
Crook of Devon, Scotland

Purpose

To involve people in the discussion of cultural origins and background in a low risk, engaging, and instructive way

Target audience

This is a good opening exercise for a group starting a training program. It is useful for groups ranging in size from six people up to the capacity of the room.

Time

20 minutes or more, depending on the size of the group and the number of questions to which you ask the group to respond

Materials and environment

- A large world map, preferably the *Peters Projection World Map* (see the Resources listing)
- Flipchart and markers
- A large open area

Procedure

Put the map on the floor in the middle of the room. Ask the group to stand around it. (If using the *Peters Map*, give them some background about how it changes our perspective of the world. The materials that come with the *Peters Map* can help you with this.)

Ask people to use the map as a guide and place themselves in the room at the place where they were born. Invite them to observe where people are standing, introduce themselves, make remarks, and ask one another questions about their background. You can also do the exercise in several stages (ask them to move from where they were born to where they live now, to where they would like to live, etc.).

Debrief

1. Ask the group what they learned and observed by doing the exercise. Note significant learnings on the flipchart and hang it in the room as a further conversation piece during the rest of the program.

2. If you are using the *Peters Map*, point out at the last debriefing that if we used other common kinds of maps (Mercator Projection, etc.), people would have been standing in different parts of the room. Maps often place our own culture in the center and others at the edge.

3. Note this improvement over having people stand in the room based on where they were born in the United States—where "foreigners" stand on the edges. (Americans in the United States are actually on the western edge of the *Peters Map*, not the center.) Of course, in other countries, a similar ethnocentric sense prevails.

Resources

The Peters Projection World Map was produced with the support of the United Nations Development Program through Friendship Press in New York.

World Map: Peters Projection. Copyright Akademische Verlagsanstalt

④ Celebrations

Selma Myers, Intercultural Development
San Diego, California, USA
and Jonamay Lambert, Lambert Associates
Hoffman Estates, Illinois, USA

Purpose

- To help participants understand the meaning of holidays practiced by diverse peoples and countries

- To explore how these observances can affect the global workplace, as well as interpersonal business relations

Target audience

This activity is richer when used with large groups of diverse participants. It is especially useful for people living and working in countries other than their own. It will also help business people in their own country when they are affected by local or national celebrations of other countries. It is a high-energy activity that gets people engaged quickly and in an enjoyable way.

Time

30 minutes

Materials and environment

- Flipchart and markers
- Handout 1, "Celebrations and You," for each participant
- Handout 2, "Holidays Around the World," for each participant
- Handout 3, "Create an International Calendar of Holidays," for each participant

Procedure

1. Distribute Handout 1, "Celebrations and You," and tell participants to answer the three questions on that page. Allow 5 to 10 minutes.

2. Pair up participants and ask them to spend 10 minutes sharing their responses on the handout with their partners.

3. Reconvene the large group and ask these questions, putting them on a flipchart or overhead for all to see:

- *What holidays were discussed? Were there any surprises?*

- *Why is it important to know about other people's holidays when working with them?*

- *How does knowledge about diverse holidays affect a business relationship? The workplace?*

- *Give specific examples of work-related situations, negative or positive, affected by differences in celebrations. What happened in each of those situations?*

- *How do you feel about holidays that are different from your own? If you had to change a scheduled meeting because someone was not able to attend due to a religious holiday or if a business you do business with was closed for a holiday that your business does not observe, what would you do?*

4. Distribute and review Handout 2. Instruct each small group to create a list of holidays, either for their own or another culture. Distribute Handout 3. Ask them to list the holidays they discussed in the appropriate months. Discuss and note holidays that are observed in different months because a lunar calendar or other reckoning of time or seasons is used.

5. Reconvene the whole group. Ask participants to tell how many holidays they came up with and ask them to give examples of how these holidays might impact them in business. Encourage participants to take these sheets home and continue to develop their own international holiday calendar. Remind them that being aware of holidays and important dates helps them learn about other cultures.

Debrief

Sum up the activity. While the handout "Holidays around the World" lists a number of important days, emphasize that people working in a global environment need to find out as much as they can about the cultures they interact with on a daily basis, and especially about how holidays impact teamwork. The more they know, the better the working relationship across cultures can become.

[Handout 1]

Celebrations and You

1. List the holidays that are most important in your life.

_____

_____

_____

_____

_____

_____

2. List other holidays different from your own that you are aware of, and write a sentence or two about them.

_____

_____

_____

_____

_____

_____

_____

_____

_____

_____

_____

3. What role do you think these holidays play when it comes to working with people from other countries, or when you are in an international work environment? How do holidays impact work?

_____

_____

_____

_____

_____

_____

[Handout 2 – page 1]

Holidays Around the World*

Learning about holidays helps people from different cultures understand one another's customs, beliefs, and traditions. By exploring holidays, one can become sensitive to the history, politics, and religion of different groups.

It is impossible to list all the holidays in the world here, but it is important for individuals who work with people from other cultures to recognize the impact that celebrations have. For example, some holidays require that those observing them refrain from working or for businesses to be closed. Some are private, while others call for fasting or feasting. Some observances invite visitors from other cultures and backgrounds as guests, while others do not.

Different Cultures, Different Years

Understanding how time is measured by different cultures will help you understand this sample list of holidays around the world. The Gregorian calendar year begins in January and defines the year as twelve months with 365 days. Each month, except February, has 30 or 31 days. A day is added to February every fourth year. Other cultures start the year at different times. *Tishri* is the first month of the Jewish calendar.

The numbering of the year can also differ. The Gregorian system records years from the traditional date of the birth of Jesus. The Jewish calendar counts years from the date of the world's creation, as determined by scholars in the fourth century. Muslims start counting years from the prophet Mohammed's flight from Mecca to Medina. Hindus count from the Saka era of Emperor Salivahana.

Islamic, Jewish, and most Asian and Hindu calendars do not have calendar years that are 365 or 366 days long because they are based on lunar calendars. None of their celebrations, including the New Year, correspond to a fixed date in the Gregorian calendar. The Jewish calendar is a solar-lunar calendar and has six different year lengths. Over long periods, the Jewish calendar averages about 365.25 days per year. The Islamic calendar averages either 354 or 355 days. Since it is always shorter than the Gregorian year, it is possible for two Islamic New Year observances to fall in a single Gregorian year.

A list of examples of holidays celebrated around the world follows.

_____

*Information in this handout is drawn from the *Year 2000 Calendar of Multicultural Celebrations & Foods,* adapted with permission of Dr. Richard Alpert. To order this annual calendar, contact Diversity Resources, 6 University Drive, Suite 206 PMB 122, Amherst, MA 01002-3820, 800-865-5549; www.diversityresources.com, RTA@amedpub.com.

Historical Observances

Most countries observe some type of annual independence day or national holiday having historical and political significance. For example:

- Independence Day, July 4th – USA
- Bastille Day – France
- Anniversary of the May Revolution – Argentina
- Restoration of Statehood Day – Armenia
- National Day – Austria
- Emancipation Day – Bahamas
- *Cinco de Mayo* – Mexico
- Veterans Day – USA

Religious Observances

Many countries or cultures within countries celebrate holidays to mark religious events or practices. In some cases, these celebrations extend over several days or more. For example:

- Islamic Ramadan
- *Eid al-Fitr* (The feast of breaking the fast of Ramadan)
- Chinese New Year
- Easter
- Three Kings Day

Saints' Days and the Birth or Death of Other Important People

- St. Patrick's Day – Ireland, Irish Americans
- Martin Luther King, Jr. Day – USA
- Buddha's birth – Buddhist communities worldwide
- Confucius' birthday – Chinese communities worldwide

Special Calendar Holidays

Some holidays have been created to celebrate important values and to recognize groups of people. For example:

- Thanksgiving Day – Canada and USA (on different days)
- Mother's Day and Father's Day – USA
- Children's Day – Japan
- Valentine's Day – USA, UK, and increasingly in other countries

Reproduced from *Reproducible Diversity and Culture Icebreakers,* by Jonamay Lambert, Selma Myers, and George Simons, editors. Amherst, MA: HRD Press, 2014

Create an International
Calendar of Holidays

Jot down as many different cultural observances as you can for each month, and ways you can integrate this information into your diversity efforts.

January: _____

_____

_____

February: _____

_____

_____

March: _____

_____

_____

April: _____

_____

_____

May: _____

_____

_____

June: _____

_____

_____

July: _____

_____

_____

August: _____

_____

_____

September: _____

_____

_____

October: _____

_____

_____

November: _____

_____

_____

December: _____

_____

_____

Other: _____

_____

_____

⑤ Identity

Steve Kulich, Shanghai International Studies University
Shanghai, China

Purpose and objectives

- To provide a simple process that helps participants become aware of their own cultural identities

- To enable participants to get to know one another more deeply than in traditional icebreakers by having them reflect individually and interact with one another

- To establish what members of the group have in common, and build a sense of teamwork

- To help participants realize and appreciate what is unique about themselves and one another as they start to work together

- To clarify the expectations that group members might have about one another and about the trainer

Target audience

The activity is effective with new or ongoing groups and can be adapted for use in various types of business, government, or classroom training. It is equally useful with homogenous or diverse groups of 4 to 20 persons.

Time

15 to 45 minutes, depending on your training objectives, level of explanation, and amount of group interaction. Suggested flow:

- Handout 1: "My Identity: Worksheet"—explanation, personal work, and discussion in pairs (15 minutes)

- Group discussion of *commonalities* and *differences* (15 minutes)

- Clarification of individual and group *expectations* of one another and the trainer (15 minutes)

Materials and environment

One copy of "My Identity: Worksheet" for each participant

Procedure

Using the "My Identity: Worksheet" (15 minutes)

1. Set up the exercise.

   - Introduce the key concepts:

     "When we come into contact with others, we often ask ourselves, 'Who are these people? What do I expect of them? Who am I to them? Can I meet their expectations of me?' Most of these questions are rooted in how we see ourselves (our identity) and how we see others (their identity).

     "Each person's identity is complex. You can see that your group leader is a man or woman and probably a trainer (public). But you have no idea about this person's marital status, exact age, salary, or other personal information. You wouldn't even dare to guess how he or she is feeling about leading this session, whether problems at home are clouding his or her thinking, or whether this person is insecure or fearful.

     "Sharing what we know about our own identities and what we would like others to know helps those around us know us better and enables us to work together better. To do this, we will use a short activity."

     (Hand out the "Identity" worksheet.)

   - Introduce the "My Identity: Worksheet" and explain each section:

     Section A. My Identity: "Take a few minutes to think about the identities that are most important to you. Let me give you an example." Create your own example. The author of the exercise has created this one: *"If you were to ask my father about his identity, he might say: (1) I'm a farmer, (2) I'm a Christian, (3) I'm the father of two children, (4) I'm an American, (5) I'm a former sailor (served in the military), (6) I'm from Kansas, (7) I vote Republican."*

     "As you can see, this person's list is a mix of public, private, and psychological dimensions."

     Review your own example with them to make sure they have the concept.

     "Take 2 to 3 minutes to think about five identities that you believe are most important to you. Write them on the sheet now. These might include your ethnicity or nationality, geographic home, educational background, profession, career achievements, current job, gender, sexual orientation, marital status or family role, religious beliefs, political orientation, specialized skills, hobbies, family name or ancestry, and personality type. There are many sources of identity. Think of five."

- Sort the list.

    "Take a moment to reflect on what you have written. How would you categorize each identity? For example, is it a vocational identity? A religious identity? A relational identity? Jot down how you might classify each of the five areas you listed."

    Section B. Shared Identities: "In the next section, jot down the first three identities that come to your mind when you think about how you are like other people or what you have in common with them. These identities might already be in Section A, or you might have just thought of them."

    Section C. Unique Identities: "What makes you unique or different from others? List at least three identities that distinguish you or set you apart and make you different from others. Again, you can pull from the first five, or add new items."

2. Have participants share with a partner. Tell them the following:

   - "Pair up with a person near you. Briefly tell your partner what the first two identities you wrote in each section mean to you or why they are important to you. After each of you share from your lists, talk about what you both have in common and how you might be different."

   - "Find a second partner and again briefly review your top two identities with this person, looking for commonalities and differences."

     A 15-minute activity could end here with a brief input from the trainer: "Now that you've gotten to know two members of the group better, let's give you a chance to know me as the group facilitator. What identities do you think might be important to me?"

     Highlight your primary identities. If this is the end of the session, sum up the exercise.

Group Reports (15 minutes)

1. **Commonalities.** "In discussing your identities with your two partners, what did you have in common?" (Record these on a flipchart.) "Did any other pairs have these same items? What items seem important to most members of this group? Why do you think those things are important?" (If the group is very diverse, you might need to probe for common areas, or direct them to write them down in Section B.) "Given these common identities, what do you think this group might enjoy talking about or doing together?"

2. **Differences.** "Take a minute to reflect on your lists and your discussion. What identity would you like to share with this group that distinguishes you from others? Jot this down in Section D."

   When they are finished, invite each person to mention one item.

From Identity to Expectations (15 minutes)

1. Introduce this part of the activity:

    "We know one another a bit better now, but knowing who we are naturally leads to what we expect of others and ourselves. Once I am aware of who I am and who you are, I naturally begin to expect that you will respond or behave in certain ways."

2. Discuss individual expectations:

    "On the back of your identity worksheet, please write out (E) two or three expectations that you have of yourself in this group; (F) two or three expectations that you have of the group itself; and (G) at least one expectation you have of the trainer." Allow 2 to 3 minutes. Give an example or two from your own expectations of yourself and of the group to make sure that participants understand what expectations are.

3. Discuss group expectations:

    "Let's look at our expectations. What can we do as a group to fulfill those expectations?" List, discuss, and set group goals for the training event.

Debrief

Summarize some of the points that show the common ground that exists in the group and some of the diverse dimensions that each group member will need to be both aware and tolerant of if they are to work well together. You might ask, "Where do you think it will be easy to communicate and work together?" and "What issues do you think will require more effort on our part to create understanding and collaboration?"

Further resources

Marshall Singer, *Perception and Identity in Intercultural Communication*. Intercultural Press, 1998.

Craig Storti, *Figuring Foreigners Out—A Practical Guide*. Intercultural Press, 1999.

William Gudykunst, *Communicating with Strangers*. Sage, 1996.

My Identity: Worksheet

A. If asked to define yourself, what words would you use? What nouns best describe your identity? Some identities describe our

- **public self** (what others can see);
- **private self** (what we seldom reveal); and
- **psychological self** (core personality, values, self-view, emotions).

What identities are most central to who or what *you* are?

List 5 identities that are very important to you. When you have found and written them down, rank them. Number 1 would be the most important, number 2 next, then number 3, and so on.

My Core Identities	Rank	Category

Now, next to each identity, write a **category** that best describes it. Is your identity most **related to** race, ethnicity, or nationality? To a geographic home—an urban or a rural location? To your educational background, career, job title, professional achievement? To gender, sexual orientation, marital status, or family role? To religious belief or political affiliation? To a special skill or capability? To a hobby or sport interest? To family name or ancestry? To personality type or other descriptive categories?

B. Some identities relate to how we **connect with others**—what we share in common. Which of your identities reflect points of connection that you share with others?

1) _____

2) _____

3) _____

[Handout 1 – page 2]

C. Some identities define how we are **unique from others.** Which of your identities distinguishes you from others? Write as many as you think apply to you.

    1) _____

    2) _____

    3) _____

D. What do you think is **the most important aspect** someone else **should know** about you? (Write a phrase or very brief statement.)

    You should know that I am...

    _____

E. Two or three self-expectations:

    1) _____

    2) _____

    3) _____

F. Two or three group expectations:

    1) _____

    2) _____

    3) _____

G. At least one trainer expectation:

    1) _____

    2) _____

⑥ Insider–Outsider

Donna Stringer, Executive Diversity Services, Inc.
Seattle, Washington, USA

Purpose

To help participants understand the following:

- We all experience being both an "insider" and an "outsider."

- Insider feelings and behaviors tend to be positive and lead to good teamwork. (Exception: Insiders can become bored because they are too much like everyone else.)

- Outsider feelings and behaviors tend to be more negative and tend to interfere with teamwork. (Exception: Outsiders can feel unique or special—especially if they and others value their differences.)

- We don't have to be, look, or act alike in order to feel included.

- Using empathy—remembering how we felt as an outsider—can make us more effective in helping someone who feels like an outsider to start feeling included.

Target audience

This activity targets most groups addressing intercultural and diversity issues. It is particularly useful for groups that are beginning to work together or that are experiencing insider–outsider stress because of reorganization, merging, etc. This activity has been used with up to 30 participants, but could probably work with larger groups.

Time

30 to 60 minutes, depending on the time allowed for identifying specific actions that create insider feelings

Materials

Two flipcharts and markers

Procedure

Prepare two flipcharts. Label one "Different" and the other "Similar." Draw a vertical line down the middle of each. Label the left side "Feelings" and the right side "Behaviors."

You say and do   We are going to do an exercise that will help us experience what it feels like to be both an outsider and an insider. I want you to begin by thinking of a time when you were in a team or a group and you felt different from others in the group. *(Pause)* Now, think of a word that describes how you felt at that time. *(Pause)* In a minute, I am going to ask you to get up and walk around the room, introducing yourself to as many people as possible, using that word. *(Alternatively, if you are short on time: In a minute, I am going to ask you to turn to your neighbors and introduce yourself using that word.)* For example, I might say to you *(walk up to someone in the classroom and shake their hand)* "Hi! I'm awkward." Okay, you may now get up *(turn to your neighbors)* and introduce yourself.

You do   Give people about 60 seconds to move around and introduce themselves, or to turn to their neighbors and introduce themselves. After 60 seconds, ask them to return to their seats or return their attention to you.

You say   Okay, whom did you meet? Call out the words you heard.

You do   As people call out the words, record them in the "Feeling" column of the "Different" flipchart. Note: If you have a training partner, he or she can do the recording so that you can attend to the participants and what they are saying. When they seem to be out of words, move to the next step.

You say   Now I want you to think of a time when you were in a team or group and felt similar to others. Identify a word that describes how you felt at that time. This time, without getting up or introducing yourselves to others, simply call out the words that come to your mind.

You do   Record (or have your partner record) the words you hear on the left side of the "Similar" chart. When participants appear to be out of words, return to the first chart.

You say and do   Let's go back to the "Different" page. When you felt like you were different and felt like these words *(quickly read through the list of feelings on the "Different" chart),* how did you act? What did you do? Call them out. *(You or your partner should record these words in the "Behavior" column of the "Different" chart.)*

That's quite a list of words. Let's label this chart "Outsiders." *(Write "Outsider" at the top of the chart near the "Different" title.)*

You say and do   Okay, let's return to this page. *(Move to the "Similar" flipchart.)* And how did you behave when you were experiencing these feelings? *(Read through the words quickly. Get them to call out the behaviors they exhibited. Write their words on the right side of this flipchart.)* Let's label this chart "Insiders." *(Write "Insider" at the top of the chart near the "Similar" title.)*

You do and say	*(Step back from the flipcharts and ask the group for their observations.)* What do you notice about these two sets of feelings and behaviors? *(Let them answer—look for the fact that outsiders are mostly negative and insiders are mostly positive; you might also hear that the outsider list is longer—if so, make the point that it is usually longer because negative experiences tend to stay with us longer, while the insider feelings tend to be simply "normal" and we don't take much notice of them.)*
You do and say	Which sets of feelings and behaviors would you want in a member of your work team? *(Let them answer.)*
	Do you need to look alike, talk alike, and think alike to have these feelings and exhibit these behaviors? *(Let them answer.)*
	If we do not need to look alike, talk alike, or think alike to feel like insiders, what are some specific things we can *do* to help people feel like insiders to the organization? *(Allow them to offer some suggestions.)*
	If you are working with a group larger than 30 or if you have more time and the workshop is intended to formulate organizational actions, put people in smaller groups of 3 to 5 persons and give them 15 minutes to identify one to three specific actions for creating insider feelings. Ask each group to report their ideas and put them on the flipchart.
You do	Listen to suggestions and observations made by the group. Allow the time to determine when you need to cut off discussion/suggestions. Give yourself 1 to 3 minutes at the end to summarize what you have just done and why. Be sure that you include the points in the Purpose (above) and Debrief (below) as you prepare your summary and transition back to your training partner.

Note: You might get some negative feelings in the "Similar" category and some positive words in the "Different" category. Use this to point out that there are positives and negatives in both experiences, but that the preponderance of feelings and behaviors is positive when we feel like others and negative when we are different.

Debrief

When debriefing, you might wish to underscore these conclusions about similarities and differences:

1. Typically, we remember more experiences and feelings about differences than experiences and feelings about our similarity with others. This occurs because experiences of difference tend to be traumatic; when they are similar, you don't need to pay much attention to your feelings and behaviors.

2. Feelings and behaviors when we are different tend to be more negative; feelings and behaviors when we feel similar tend to be positive. (Note the exceptions above in the instructions.)

3. Feelings and behaviors when we are similar are effective team member feelings and behaviors.

4. Using empathy—remembering how we felt when we were different—can be very effective in helping us identify ways to include the person who might be feeling different (a new employee, someone who has just moved from another area or country within the organization, someone who is visibly different from others, or someone who has language challenges). When we see the behaviors of the outsider, instead of labeling the person, use empathy to ask if they are possibly feeling like an outsider.

5. We don't have to look alike, act alike, dress alike, or sound alike in order to *feel* like an insider. If our organization and coworkers value differences, they can help us feel like insiders, regardless of our differences.

⑦ Silent Interview

Donna Stringer, Executive Diversity Services, Inc.
Seattle, Washington, USA

Purpose and learning objectives
- To introduce training participants to one another
- To examine stereotypes and first impressions
- To examine what cultural assumptions people make on first meeting

Target audience

This is a good icebreaker for a diversity awareness class where participants do not know one another well. It has worked in several international groups with up to 13 national populations represented and is especially useful for making the point that stereotypes are based on visual differences.

Time

60 minutes with a group of 30 or less. Use with larger groups is not recommended because the reporting and introductions step becomes tedious if too many are in the group. It is ideal for groups of 20 or less.

Materials
- Handout 1, "Silent Interview: Process," for each participant
- Handout 2, "Interview Questions," for each participant

Procedure

1. Pair individual participants with others whom they don't know or whom they know least well.

2. Tell participants that they have 10 minutes to complete the silent interview process *about their partner.* There is to be *no talking* during this time.

3. Stress that it is okay to look at your partner during this exercise, even if you might not normally do such a thing, and that it is okay to make guesses and to be wrong.

4. When 10 minutes are up, ask the partners to share their answers with one another and obtain the accurate information.

5. Have each person introduce her or his partner to the whole group and share information about one thing they learned from the verbal interviews that took them by surprise.

6. Ask for their observations about this process. What was easy and why? What was difficult and why?

You may modify the questions to address the cultural or cross-cultural issues of greatest interest or concern among participants.

Debrief

Guide the debrief in the direction of these important conclusions:

1. First impressions, which we all have, are usually colored by our own feelings and values. Because of this, our first impressions are sometimes wrong.

2. Being asked to share those first impressions is uncomfortable because we are aware that they might be based on stereotypes and consequently be inaccurate.

3. Knowing that others are judging us is an uncomfortable feeling.

4. Our first impressions can be even more inaccurate if we are unable to ask for and receive feedback.

5. Some people are uncomfortable being the first to speak because their culture considers this impolite. For others, it might not be uncomfortable at all.

6. Assumptions are based on previous experience, as are the categories we use to assess one another.

7. We often miss important clues.

[Handout 1]

Silent Interview: Process

Instructions: Pair up with the person in this room with whom you are least familiar.

First 10 minutes: Conduct a *silent interview* with your partner.

NO TALKING!

Answer the questions on Handout 2, "Interview Questions," by looking at your partner and responding as you believe your partner would, if she or he could speak.

    a) Write your answers for each question on the lines labeled "a)".

Second 10 minutes: b) Share your presumed responses with your partner. Ask for your partner's actual responses. Discuss how you arrived at your assumptions. Write your partner's own answers to each question on the lines labeled "b)".

Brief: Back in the large group, introduce your partner by name and share the most surprising discovery you made about her or him.

[Handout 2]

Interview Questions

1. What is this person's ethnic or national group?

   a) _____

   b) _____

2. Where did this person grow up? Describe the neighborhood and the geography.

   a) _____

   b) _____

3. What does this person do in his or her spare time?

   a) _____

   b) _____

4. What would be the *ideal* gift for this person?

   a) _____

   b) _____

5. What kind of school or educational institution did this person attend?

   a) _____

   b) _____

6. Describe this person's current neighborhood: rural, suburban, or core city; busy or quiet; single home or apartment; etc.

   a) _____

   b) _____

⑧ Name that Feeling

Purpose and learning objectives

The purpose of this activity is to help participants begin to focus on what it's like to feel different.

Time

15 minutes

Materials

Flipchart and markers

Procedure

1. Ask participants to think of a time when they felt different from everyone else. For example, walking into a meeting and being the only person of one race, or the only female or the only person who spoke English.

2. Ask the participants to think of the ONE WORD that best describes how they felt at that time.

3. Instruct participants to walk around the room, introducing themselves to other participants by using, instead of their names, the ONE word they thought of that best expressed their feelings. (Give personal examples: "I once was the only hearing person in a roomful of people using sign language. I felt 'ISOLATED'." As the person shakes hands, his/her introduction is: "Hello, I'm 'ISOLATED'.")

4. After most participants have met each other, ask them to return to their seats and discuss their experiences. As the participants describe the words they used for their introduction, write the words on the flipchart. Use the following questions as guides to the discussion:

   - How did you feel? What were some of the words that were used during the introductions?

   - Were there more positive or negative words used to describe feelings?

   - In the workplace, what are the implications of the positive words? Of the negative words?

   - Does anyone want to share an experience he/she had in feeling different?

Conclusion

Close by saying that even though we all have felt "different" at one time or another it's easy to forget the feelings that are associated with it. We may unintentionally exclude others or behave in ways that send mixed messages. If we can remember our own feelings about being different, it may help us be more sensitive to others.

⑨ Diversity Letter Game

Purpose and learning objectives

The purpose of this activity is to have participants define for themselves the meaning of diversity.

Time

10 minutes

Materials

- Flipchart and markers
- Paper

Procedure

1. Show the participants the previously-prepared flipchart and explain that the group's task will be to come up with what they feel makes up diversity.

2. Group participants in pairs and ask them to think of as many words as possible for each letter, helping clarify the term "Diversity," and write them down. Tell them they have 3 minutes to complete this assignment.

3. After 3 minutes call "Stop," and ask each pair to orally report the words they chose for each letter.

4. Reconvene the group and have the participants call out their words. Record the responses on the flipchart and compare.

Conclusion

Summarize by pointing out the variety of words that the participants used to define diversity. Explain that diversity is much broader than race and gender and that the challenge is to learn how diversity impacts everyone, everywhere.

Trainer's Notes

In preparation, print the letters spelling **D I V E R S I T Y   G A M E** vertically on the flipchart, down the left side.

Most of the letters lead easily to words describing diversity. Let the participants proceed on their own, but if they need help, you may jog their thinking by using some of the following examples:

D	=	Disability; different styles
I	=	Individuals; intelligence
V	=	Varying; various; variety
E	=	Education; economic status
R	=	Race; religion
S	=	Sexual orientation; social class; similarities
I	=	Individuals; intelligence
T	=	Thought processes; team efforts; traits
Y	=	Youth; years
G	=	Gender; geographical origins
A	=	Age difference
M	=	Multicultural
E	=	Education; economic status

⑩ Who Do You Know?

Purpose and learning objectives

The purpose of this activity is to begin exploring what participants know about people from differing groups.

Time

15 minutes

Materials

- Papers and pencils
- Flipchart and markers

Procedure

1. On the flipchart list these four categories: "Author," "Artist," "Musician," "Politician." Prepare the flipchart in advance of the session.

2. Ask participants to quickly write down on their own paper five persons (living or dead) that they are familiar with for each category. Allow 5 to 10 minutes.

3. Then ask the participants to place an asterisk next to those names of the five in each category who represent someone from their own ethnic and racial group, or country they were born in.

4. Place the participants into small groups and ask them to compare their lists, the names they wrote and the number of people they starred. Ask them to discuss whether race, ethnicity or country of origin played a role in their choices. If so, why? If not, why not?

5. Reconvene and ask them to orally report the results of their discussions.

6. Discuss what conclusions can be drawn from this exercise. Were women or people of color listed? If so, by whom? Did the categories themselves make a difference?

Conclusion

Close by saying that often we're more comfortable with similarities and know more about people we have been exposed to. Much of our comfort level is based on when and where we grew up, as well as other personal influences such as parents, schools, churches, the media, etc.

⑪ Time Marches On

Purpose and learning objectives

The purpose of this activity is to help participants understand how one's values change over time.

Time

15–20 minutes

Materials

Papers and pencils

Procedure

1. Explain to the group that this is a written reflective exercise. Ask the participants to think about themselves at the present time and have them answer the question, "What *are* my present beliefs, attitudes and values about people of other races or ethnic groups?" Then have them take a few minutes to write what comes to mind.

2. Next, have them think about themselves 10 years ago. Have them answer the question, "What *were* my beliefs, attitudes and values about people of other races or ethnic groups?" Then have them take a few minutes to write what comes to mind.

3. Ask them to think about and compare their answers about the present time with their past attitudes, and discuss what similarities they sensed and what changes occurred.

4. Place the participants into small groups and have them discuss among themselves the responses to the first two questions.

5. Ask them to discuss how they would like their beliefs, attitudes and values about people of other races or ethnic groups to be *in the future, perhaps in 7 years.* Reconvene and have the groups report aloud.

Conclusion

Sum up the various comments of the group and point out that beliefs and attitudes may change over time.

⓬ Back to the Future

Purpose and learning objectives

The purpose of this activity is to give the participants the opportunity to look at diversity issues in their past and share them with other participants.

Time

15–20 minutes

Materials

- Crayons or colored pencils
- Paper
- Flipchart and markers

Procedure

1. Ask the participants to draw a picture of themselves from their past, at a time when they had their first experience with diversity.

2. Divide participants into groups of four or five and ask them to discuss their drawings, and the similarities and differences in their early experiences.

3. Reconvene and have them orally report on what kinds of experiences were similar and what kinds were different. Record the responses on a flipchart.

Conclusion

Early experiences have a major influence on the way people interact with one another; many of their reactions, when facing diversity issues, come from early experiences. They have to decide whether they have changed, and whether they have the capacity to change even more.

Trainer's Notes

It's a good idea for trainers to begin by drawing their own picture as an example.

⓭ Into the Future

Purpose and learning objectives

The purpose of this activity is to give the participants the opportunity to think about themselves as being old and share their thoughts with other participants.

Time

15–20 minutes

Materials

- Crayons or colored pencils
- Paper
- Flipchart and markers

Procedure

1. Ask the participants to draw a future picture of themselves as they think of what they will be like and what they may be doing when they are over the age of 70.

2. Divide participants into groups of four or five and ask them to share their drawings. Ask them to discuss what their expectations of the future were based on. They can then discuss the similarities and differences of the sources of their expectations, with particular attention to how they think they will be treated by younger people.

3. Reconvene and have them orally report on their discussions. Ask them to call out the various ways that older people are often treated, and record the responses on the flipchart.

Conclusion

Today, people live longer than ever before. Indeed, this generation is the first one able to look ahead, picture themselves as they might be, and perhaps make a difference.

This activity may also lead to a discussion of how older people are treated in society today, and realize that "ageism" is as offensive as any of the other "ism's."

Trainer's Notes

It's a good idea for trainers to begin by drawing their own picture as an example.

⑭ Cultural Hat Dance

Purpose and learning objectives

The purpose of this activity is to have participants understand perception and to get them thinking creatively.

Time

10–15 minutes

Materials

- A variety of different hats; enough to assign one to each discussion group
- Paper and pencils

Procedure

1. Divide the participants into discussion groups of four or five and give a hat to each group. (See Trainer's Notes for hat suggestions.)

2. Ask participants to write a description of the person who would wear the hat. You can use the stem statement, "The hat belongs to..." and then have them thoroughly describe that person.

3. Have the participants in each group compare their written comments, and note similarities and differences.

4. Reconvene and have each group orally report on the similarities and differences of opinion within their groups.

Conclusion

Close by stating there are many ways to view the same object. Our experiences influence how we view things.

Trainer's Notes

Before the session, assemble a collection of hats of various types, such as hard hats, straw hats, baseball caps, ladies' dress hats, turbans, bicycle helmets, etc., with at least one hat for each discussion group.

⓯ Take Your Pick—Learning Styles

Purpose and learning objectives

The purpose of this activity is to help participants understand that there are differences in learning styles and to identify their own learning style.

Time

10 minutes

Materials

- Pen
- Book
- Audio cassette and video cassette

Procedure

1. Place the following four objects on the desk: pen, book, audio cassette and video cassette.

2. Ask participants to choose for themselves the object that is most interesting to them.

3. Group participants in pairs and ask them to share their responses and discuss why they made that choice.

4. Reconvene and ask the following questions.

   - Why did you choose the object you did?

   - Did you realize (or discuss) that each object represented a different learning style?

   - In your discussion with your partner, what did you find out about that person?

   - How did you feel sharing this type of personal information? Did you discover more about your own learning style?

   - What are the benefits of knowing more about the learning styles of people you are dealing with?

Conclusion

Diversity also may incorporate learning style differences. The more you know about the people you are working with, the better the communication and interaction will be.

⑯ Political Savvy

Purpose and learning objectives

The purpose of this activity is to enable participants to determine the most effective qualities for leadership for multicultural groups.

Time

15–20 minutes

Materials

Flipchart and markers

Procedure

1. Group participants in pairs and explain that one of the two will be running for the President of a county-wide Council for Equality, a position that requires effective leadership of diverse groups and an understanding of a multicultural community. The other person will be the campaign manager. Ask each pair to decide who will take on which role.

2. It will be the task of the campaign manager to introduce the candidate, promote that individual for President of the Council for Equality, and try to get the candidate elected.

3. Ask each pair to discuss the characteristics or qualities they believe are needed to win the election. Together, they can plan the introduction, and a strategy that would be most helpful in winning the election.

4. Reconvene and ask each of the campaign managers to make a pitch for his or her candidate.

5. Record the important characteristics and qualities on the flipchart.

6. Lead a discussion with questions such as:

   - What were the qualities most often included by the campaign managers?
   - Which qualities do you think are most important to be an effective leader of a multicultural group? Discuss the top three or four.
   - How are these qualities different from the norms of accepted leadership in general?
   - How did the campaign managers present their candidates? Did you notice different styles? If so, what were they?

Conclusion

Point out that there is a core group of leadership qualities that any effective leader needs. However, when dealing across cultures there are additional factors that need to be considered, as noted in the discussion.

Trainer's Notes

Here is a chance to explore some assumptions that may have been made by the campaign managers in planning their presentations:

- All of the voters speak and understand English.

- There are no hearing impaired citizens in attendance.

- Learning styles are the same.

Head in the Clouds, Nose to the Grindstone

17

Purpose and learning objectives

The purpose of this activity is to help participants become aware of the tremendous amount of slang used regularly in English conversation and to realize that communicating with non-native speakers of English may take extra effort.

Time

15–20 minutes

Materials

- Paper and pencils
- Flipchart and markers

Procedure

1. Introduce the topic of slang by explaining that it is always present in normal conversation. Ask participants to jot down all the "socially acceptable" slang terms they use or have heard others use in the following categories, as shown on the flipchart (which the trainer prepares in advance).

   - Sports
   - Western or cowboy talk
   - Clothing
   - Parts of the body

2. If the group needs help getting started, you might give examples such as:

   - Sports—"ballpark figure," "a knockout"
   - Western or cowboy talk—"shoot from the hip," "ride herd on"
   - Parts of the body—"elbow grease," "shake a leg"
   - Clothing—"given the boot," "shirt off his back"

3. Divide participants into small groups and have them compare the phrases they wrote. Ask them to think about and discuss the amount of slang they use in everyday conversation and where some of these expressions came from. They can also share any experiences they have had either not understanding slang or not being understood when they used it.

4. Reconvene and ask participants to orally report on the category that had the most slang phrases. Record the number on the prepared flipchart that lists the categories.

5. Ask the group to call out some of the most commonly used expressions as well as those they felt were the most difficult for someone who did not grow up speaking English. (You may want to add these to the flipchart.)

6. Open the discussion to the possible problems using too much slang and gather some ideas about what people can do to help a non-native speaker.

Conclusion

Summarize with the fact that it is difficult to realize how much slang Americans use. Point out that the use of slang can be a serious barrier to good communication in general. In fact, often any listener may not have the same slang vocabulary that the speaker has and consequently will not fully understand.

It is important to be sensitive to the fact people who grew up speaking another language may not understand a conversation when there is a lot of slang. Often they are too embarrassed to ask and so go along as if they understand. (As for what people can do, perhaps monitoring their own use of slang and checking for understanding is the best solution.)

Slang also differs in various parts of the United States, and during different time periods.

Trainer's Notes

In the case of non-native English speaking participants, they can contribute by citing English slang expressions where the meanings were difficult to understand, or were misinterpreted.

In this activity, we have used the word "slang" to refer both to slang (which changes over time) and to idioms (which become embedded in the language).